THE ALL-AMERICAN
ROTISSERIE CHICKEN
Dinner

QUICK & EASY RECIPES TO
DRESS UP YOUR STORE-BOUGHT BIRD

HOPE COMERFORD
PHOTOS BY BONNIE MATTHEWS

Good ⚘ Books

New York, New York

Good Books books may be purchased in bulk at special discounts for sales
promotion, corporate gifts, fund-raising, or educational purposes. Special
editions can also be created to specifications. For details, contact the
Special Sales Department, Good Books, 307 West 36th Street, 11th Floor,
New York, NY 10018 or info@skyhorsepublishing.com.

Good Books is an imprint of Skyhorse Publishing, Inc.®, a Delaware
corporation.

Visit our website at www.goodbooks.com.

10 9 8 7 6 5 4 3 2 1

Library of Congress Cataloging-in-Publication Data is available on file.

Cover design by Daniel Brount

Print ISBN: 978-1-68099-629-6
Ebook ISBN: 978-1-68099-695-1

Printed in China

CONTENTS

ABOUT *THE ALL-AMERICAN ROTISSERIE CHICKEN DINNER*

Welcome to *The All-American Rotisserie Chicken Dinner: Quick & Easy Recipes to Dress Up Your Store-Bought Bird*. More and more home cooks are turning to store-bought, ready-to-eat rotisserie chickens for a quick and easy dinner. With the popularity rising, we thought this cookbook would make a great addition to your kitchen when you need something else to go with that delicious bird, or you don't want to eat it as is.

This book contains seventy-five recipes to help you repurpose your leftover rotisserie chicken or give you some delectable side dishes to go with it. We've got recipes for everything from Mexican Egg Rolls, Chicken Salad Roll-Ups, and White Chicken Chili Casserole to Stuffed Sweet Pepper Soup, Chicken Tortellini Soup, and Ginger Chicken Noodle Soup. We'll help you get an amazing dinner on the table in no time! So, pick yourself up a rotisserie chicken on the way home and let's make some kitchen magic happen!

ROTISSERIE CHICKEN TIPS & TRICKS

SAFE HANDLING

- Within two hours of bringing the rotisserie chicken home, be sure to refrigerate it. If it's a really hot day, refrigerate it within the hour.
- If you want to refrigerate the rotisserie chicken immediately, cut the meat off the bones first. If you're in a real time crunch, at bare minimum, break the bird in half and spread it open, then place it in the fridge.
- When purchasing your rotisserie chicken, put it in your cart last. This will ensure you get it home safely and will be more fresh when you go to eat/serve it.
- Use up the meat within four days.
- If you choose to freeze the meat, use it up within four months.

HOW TO CARVE

1. First, lay the chicken on a cutting board, breast-side up.

2. If there is any twine holding the legs together, cut and discard it.

3. Next you will pull each of the legs gently away from the body of the bird. You will cut each at the joint with a sharp knife to remove them.

4. Separate each leg piece from the thigh it's attached to by cutting through the joint with a sharp knife.

5. Gently pull the wing tip away from the body of the bird. You should now be able to slip the knife down between the wing and the breast and cut through the joint.

6. Now you can begin slicing the meat off each side of the breast, starting with the outside of the breast and working your way toward the center. From here, you can decide if you want to shred, dice, chop, or leave it as slices.

TIPS

- It is easier to separate the meat from the bone when it's warm!
- If you want to quickly shred the rotisserie chicken meat, simply place it in a deep bowl and use an electric beater to shred it!
- Save and use the bones from the rotisserie chicken to make your own broth/stock. Simply add veggies (onions, carrots, celery) and just enough water to cover it all, then bring to a boil and let it simmer for 30 minutes. Add in some of your favorite fresh herbs to make an even tastier broth.

STARTERS & SNACKS

BUFFALO CHICKEN DIP

Deb Martin
Gap, PA

Makes 8 cups
Prep. Time: 15 minutes
Cooking Time: 20–60 minutes

1¼ cups shredded rotisserie chicken meat
¼ cup Frank's RedHot Original Cayenne Pepper Sauce
2 (8-oz.) pkgs. cream cheese, softened
1 cup ranch dressing
1½–3 cups shredded cheddar jack cheese, *divided*
tortilla chips

1. Heat chicken and hot sauce in a large frying pan over medium heat until heated through.

2. Stir in cream cheese and ranch dressing. Cook, stirring, until well blended and warm.

3. Mix in half of shredded cheese.

4. Transfer the mixture to a small slow cooker. Sprinkle the remaining cheese over the top.

5. Cover and cook on Low setting until hot and bubbly. Serve with tortilla chips.

VARIATION:
Replace hot sauce with 1 cup buffalo wing sauce. Spread cream cheese in bottom of small shallow baking dish. Layer with shredded chicken, buffalo wing sauce, ranch dressing, and shredded cheese. Bake at 350°F for 20 minutes or until cheese is melted.
—Donna Treloar, Muncie, IN

MEXICAN EGG ROLLS

Brittany Miller
Millersburg, OH

Makes 18 egg rolls
Prep. Time: 35–40 minutes
Cooking Time: 5 minutes/batch; about 20 minutes total

2½ cups shredded rotisserie chicken meat
1½ cups (6-oz.) shredded Mexican cheese blend
1 cup frozen corn, thawed
1 cup canned black beans, rinsed and drained
5 green onions, chopped
¼ cup minced fresh cilantro
1 tsp. salt
1 tsp. ground cumin
1 tsp. grated lime peel
¼ tsp. cayenne powder
1 (1-lb.) package egg roll wrappers
oil for deep-fat frying

1. In large bowl, combine chicken, cheese, corn, beans, onions, cilantro, salt, cumin, lime peel, and cayenne.

2. Place ¼ cup of mixture in center of one egg roll wrapper. (Keep remaining wrappers covered with damp paper towel until ready to use.)

3. Fold bottom corner over filling. Fold sides toward the center over filling. Moisten remaining corner with water. Roll up tightly to seal. Repeat with each wrapper.

4. In electric skillet or deep-fat fryer, heat oil to 375°F. Fry egg rolls, a few at a time, for 2 minutes on each side or until golden brown.

5. Drain on paper towels.

TIPS:
1. Keep finished egg rolls warm in a covered dish until ready to serve.
2. Serve with salsa and/or sour cream as dipping sauces.
—Carna Reitz
Remington, VA

CHICKEN SALAD ROLL-UPS

F. Elaine Asper, Norton, OH

Makes 8 roll-ups
Prep. Time: 20 minutes
Cooking/Baking Time: 30 minutes

1¼ cups shredded rotisserie chicken meat
1 medium green bell pepper, finely chopped
2 Tbsp. mayonnaise
½ tsp. salt
8-oz. tube refrigerated crescent rolls
¼ cup chopped pimento, *optional*

1. In a medium-sized bowl, mix chicken, bell pepper, mayonnaise, and salt together. Set aside.

2. Grease baking sheet.

3. Separate crescents into 4 rectangles, using 2 triangles to make 1 rectangle. Press out the perforations.

4. Place 2 dough rectangles on a lightly floured surface, overlapping short sides slightly. With floured rolling pin, roll to 15 × 4 inches.

5. With spoon, spread half the chicken mix on dough, ½ inch from the edges on all sides.

6. Start at short side and roll up jelly-roll fashion. Cut into 4 equal slices. Place on cookie sheet.

7. Repeat steps 5–7 with remaining 2 dough rectangles.

8. Bake at 375°F for 30 minutes, or until golden brown.

LOADED ROTISSERIE NACHOS

Hope Comerford
Clinton Township, MI

Makes 6 servings
Prep. Time: 10 minutes
Bake Time: 10–12 minutes

1 (12-oz.) bag tortilla chips or strips
2 cups shredded rotisserie chicken meat
1 (15-oz.) can pinto beans, drained
½ cup sliced kalamata olives
½ cup diced onions
2 cups shredded cheddar cheese
2 cups shredded Monterey Jack cheese
⅓ cup sliced fresh jalapeños
1 avocado, diced
⅓ cup chopped fresh cilantro

1. Preheat the oven to 425°F.

2. Spread the tortilla chips out on a baking sheet.

3. Evenly spread the rotisserie chicken meat, pinto beans, kalamata olives, and diced onions over the top of the chips.

4. Sprinkle the cheese evenly over the top of all of the toppings.

5. Top the cheese with the fresh jalapeño slices.

6. Bake in the oven for 10–12 minutes, or until cheese is melted.

7. Top with the avocado and cilantro.

8. Serve and enjoy!

SERVING SUGGESTION:
You can always top these loaded nachos with sour cream and fresh salsa as well, or just serve it alongside.

BARBECUE CHICKEN PIZZA

Hope Comerford
Clinton Township, MI

Makes 6 servings
Prep. Time: 10 minutes
Cooking/Baking Time: 13–15 minutes

14 oz. premade or homemade pizza dough
½ cup sliced red onion pieces
1 Tbsp. olive oil
1½ cups diced rotisserie chicken meat
1½ cups of your favorite barbecue sauce, *divided*
3 cups mozzarella cheese
⅓ cup chopped fresh cilantro

1. Spread pizza dough on a pizza pan and bake for 5 minutes at whatever temperature the packaging suggests.

2. While the pizza dough is cooking, sauté the red onion pieces in the olive oil until they are translucent. Set aside.

3. When the pizza crust has finished its 5 minutes, remove it.

4. Spread ½ cup of the barbecue sauce over the pizza crust.

5. Toss the rotisserie chicken meat with the remaining barbecue sauce and arrange it on the pizza crust.

6. Arrange the sautéed red onion pieces on the pizza crust.

7. Sprinkle the mozzarella cheese evenly over the toppings on the pizza.

8. Bake the pizza for 8–10 minutes, or until the cheese is melted and crust is golden brown.

9. When you remove the pizza, sprinkle it with the cilantro.

10. Serve and enjoy!

MAIN DISHES

CREAMY CHICKEN LASAGNA

Joanne E. Martin
Stevens, PA

Makes 10 servings
Prep. Time: 30 minutes
Baking Time: 40–45 minutes

8 oz. uncooked lasagna noodles, *divided*
1 (10¾-oz.) can cream of mushroom soup
1 (10¾-oz.) can cream of chicken soup
½ cup freshly grated Parmesan cheese
1 cup sour cream
3 cups diced rotisserie chicken meat
½ cup shredded mozzarella cheese, *divided*

1. Cook noodles according to package directions in unsalted water. Drain.

2. In mixing bowl, blend together soups, Parmesan cheese, and sour cream.

3. Stir in chicken.

4. Put ¼ of chicken mixture in greased 9 × 13-inch baking pan.

5. Top with half the cooked noodles.

6. Spoon in half the chicken mixture.

7. Sprinkle with half the mozzarella cheese.

8. Repeat layers, using all remaining ingredients.

9. Bake at 350°F for 40–45 minutes, or until heated through.

CHICKEN AND BROCCOLI BAKE

Jan Rankin
Millersville, PA

Makes 12–16 servings
Prep. Time: 15 minutes
Baking Time: 30 minutes

2 (10¾-oz.) cans cream of chicken soup

2½ cups milk, *divided*

16-oz. bag frozen chopped broccoli, thawed and drained

3 cups chopped rotisserie chicken meat

2 cups buttermilk baking mix

1. Mix soup and 1 cup milk together in large mixing bowl until smooth.

2. Stir in broccoli and chicken.

3. Pour into well-greased 9x13-inch baking dish.

4. Mix together 1½ cups milk and baking mix in mixing bowl.

5. Spoon evenly over top of chicken-broccoli mixture.

6. Bake at 450°F for 30 minutes.

CHICKEN DIVAN

Linda Sluiter
Schererville, PA

Makes 4 servings
Prep. Time: 20 minutes
Baking Time: 1 hour

---

2 cups cubed rotisserie chicken meat
2 (10¾-oz.) cans cream of chicken soup
1 lb. frozen broccoli, thawed and drained
1 cup Minute Rice
2 Tbsp. butter, melted
1 cup milk
8 oz. shredded cheddar cheese

1. In large mixing bowl, stir together chicken, soup, broccoli, rice, butter, milk, and cheese.

2. Pour into greased 9x13-inch baking pan.

3. Bake, covered, at 350°F for 30 minutes.

4. Remove cover. Bake 30 more minutes.

CHICKEN ASPARAGUS BAKE

Jean Butzer
Batavia, NY

Makes 4 servings
Prep. Time: 15–20 minutes
Chilling Time: 8–24 hours
Cooking/Baking Time: 1¼ hours

¾ lb. fresh asparagus spears, or 1 (10-oz.) package frozen asparagus spears

4 Tbsp. spreadable butter, *divided*

5 Tbsp. flour

1 cup milk

1 cup low-sodium chicken broth

½ lb. fresh mushrooms, sliced, or 1 (6-oz.) can sliced mushrooms, drained

⅛ tsp. nutmeg

Dash pepper

2 cups sliced rotisserie chicken meat

¼ cup bread crumbs

2 Tbsp. snipped parsley

2 Tbsp. slivered almonds

1. Cook asparagus lightly in microwave or in a saucepan on the stovetop. Drain.

2. In a skillet or saucepan, melt 2 Tbsp. spreadable butter. Blend in flour.

3. Whisk in milk and chicken broth. Cook, stirring constantly, until mixture is thickened and bubbly.

4. Stir in mushrooms, nutmeg, and pepper.

5. Arrange chicken slices in bottom of lightly greased 6×10-inch baking pan.

6. Spoon half of mushroom sauce over chicken.

7. Arrange asparagus over sauce.

8. Pour remaining sauce over asparagus spears.

9. Cover and refrigerate up to 24 hours.

10. In a bowl, toss bread crumbs, parsley, almonds, and 2 Tbsp. spreadable butter together. Set aside.

11. Bake casserole, covered, for 30 minutes at 375°F.

12. Remove cover. Sprinkle crumbs on top.

13. Bake, uncovered, until heated through, about 15 minutes longer.

CREAMY CHICKEN & SPINACH CASSEROLE

Laverne Nafziger
Goshen, IN

Makes 6 servings
Prep. Time: 15–20 minutes
Baking Time: 35–40 minutes

¾ cup mayonnaise

¾ cup yogurt

½ cup sour cream

1 cup shredded cheddar cheese

1 tsp. minced garlic

1½ cups diced rotisserie chicken meat

1 (10-oz.) package frozen chopped spinach, thawed and squeezed dry

¾ cup crushed cracker crumbs

⅔ cup grated Parmesan cheese

1. In a good-sized mixing bowl, blend together mayonnaise, yogurt, sour cream, cheddar cheese, and garlic.

2. Stir in chicken and spinach.

3. Spoon into buttered 6½×8½-inch baking dish.

4. In mixing bowl, stir together cracker crumbs and Parmesan cheese.

5. Sprinkle over top.

6. Bake at 350°F for 35–40 minutes, or until topping is lightly browned and mixture is bubbly.

CHICKEN SPECTACULAR

Rebecca Meyerkorth
Wamego, KS
Melissa Wenger
Orrville, OH

Makes 12 servings
Prep. Time: 30 minutes
Baking Time: 30 minutes
Standing Time: 5 minutes

1 (6-oz.) package Uncle Ben's Long Grain and Wild Rice
3 cups diced rotisserie chicken meat
1 (10¾-oz.) can cream of celery soup
1 medium jar chopped pimentos, drained
1 medium onion, chopped
1 (15-oz.) can green beans, French-cut style, drained
1 cup mayonnaise
½–1 tsp. Worcestershire sauce, according to your taste preference
¼ tsp. pepper
1 (8-oz.) can sliced water chestnuts, drained
1 cup grated cheddar cheese

1. Prepare rice according to package directions.

2. Put prepared rice in large bowl. Add chicken, soup, pimentos, onion, beans, mayonnaise, Worcestershire sauce, pepper, and water chestnuts. Mix.

3. Pour into greased 9×13-inch baking dish.

4. Bake at 350°F for 30 minutes, or until bubbly and heated through.

5. Sprinkle with cheese. Let stand 5 minutes for cheese to melt

TIP:
You can prepare through Step 3 and then freeze until needed.

SIMMERING CHICKEN DINNER

Trish Dick
Ladysmith, WI

Makes 4 servings
Prep. Time: 10 minutes

2½ cups chicken broth
½ cup apple juice
1 bay leaf
½ tsp. garlic powder
½ tsp. paprika
¼ tsp. salt
2½ cups chopped rotisserie chicken meat
1 cup uncooked whole-grain rice
3 cups fresh, or frozen, vegetables—your choice of one, or a mix
½ tsp. paprika, *optional*
parsley as garnish, *optional*

1. Heat chicken broth, apple juice, bay leaf, garlic powder, paprika, and salt in large skillet until boiling, stirring occasionally.

2. Add chicken. Cover. Reduce heat and simmer 10 minutes on low.

3. Turn chicken.

4. Add 1 cup rice around chicken.

5. Top with the vegetables.

6. Cover. Simmer 25 minutes, or until rice is cooked, vegetables are as soft as you like, and chicken is done.

7. Remove bay leaf.

8. Sprinkle with paprika and parsley before serving if you wish.

TIP:
If you like a bit of zip, add curry powder in place of paprika.

CHICKEN RICE CASSEROLE

Alma Yoder
Baltic, OH

Makes 8 servings
Prep. Time: 20 minutes
Baking Time: 45 minutes

2 cups uncooked long-grain rice
4 cups chicken broth
2 cups diced celery
2 Tbsp. butter
1 (10¾-oz.) can mushroom soup
1½ cups mayonnaise
2 Tbsp. chopped onion
2 cups cubed rotisserie chicken meat
2 cups crushed cornflakes
2 Tbsp. butter, melted

1. In large saucepan, cook rice in chicken broth, covered, for about 20 minutes over low heat.

2. While rice is cooking, sauté celery in butter in skillet.

3. When rice is tender, add celery, soup, mayonnaise, onion, and chicken to rice. Mix gently.

4. Spoon mixture into greased casserole dish.

5. Mix crushed cornflakes and melted butter together in small bowl.

6. Scatter cornflake mixture on top.

7. Bake, covered, at 350°F for 30 minutes.

8. Uncover. Bake 15 more minutes, or until bubbly and heated through.

CHICKEN CORDON BLEU CASSEROLE

Marcia S. Myer
Manheim, PA
Rachel King
Castile, NY

Makes 20–24 servings
Prep. Time: 30 minutes
Baking Time: 1 hour

Filling:
1½ cups diced celery
1 small onion, chopped
3 Tbsp. butter
8 cups cubed bread
2 eggs
1¾ cups milk
½ tsp. salt
¼ tsp. pepper

1 lb. chipped ham
½ lb. grated Swiss cheese
3 cups diced rotisserie chicken meat
1 (10¾-oz.) can cream of chicken soup
½ cup milk

TIP:
This makes a lot. You can always
freeze one baking dish and defrost
and cook another day.

1. Prepare filling by sautéing celery and onion in butter in saucepan until soft.

2. Place cubed bread in large mixing bowl.

3. Pour sautéed vegetables, eggs, 1¾ cups milk, salt, and pepper over bread.

4. Grease 2 9×13-inch baking pans.

5. Layer half of ham, cheese, and filling into each pan.

6. Layer half of chicken into each pan, distributing evenly over top of filling mixture.

7. In mixing bowl, blend soup and ½ cup milk together.

8. Pour soup mixture over top of chicken.

9. Bake at 350°F for 60 minutes.

CHICKEN NOODLE CASSEROLE

Leesa DeMartyn
Enola, PA

Makes 4–6 servings
Prep. Time: 15–20 minutes
Baking Time: 30 minutes

1 Tbsp. butter
¼ cup chopped onion
¼ cup chopped green bell pepper
1 (8-oz.) package egg noodles, cooked and drained
2 cups cubed rotisserie chicken meat
1 medium tomato, peeled and chopped
1 Tbsp. lemon juice
¼ tsp. salt
¼ tsp. pepper
½ cup mayonnaise
⅓ cup milk
½ cup shredded cheddar cheese
bread crumbs, *optional*

1. Melt butter in small skillet over medium heat.

2. Sauté onion and bell pepper for about 5 minutes.

3. In large mixing bowl, combine onion and pepper with cooked noodles, chicken, tomato, lemon juice, salt, pepper, mayonnaise, and milk.

4. Turn into greased 2-quart casserole.

5. Top with cheese, and bread crumbs if you wish.

6. Cover with foil. Bake at 400°F for 30 minutes, or until heated through.

7. Let stand 10 minutes before serving to allow sauce to thicken.

CHICKEN SUPREME

Janet Suderman
Indianapolis, IN

Makes 6 servings
Prep. Time: 15 minutes
Cooking Time: about 20 minutes

2 cups sliced fresh mushrooms
1 small onion, chopped
1 cup thinly sliced celery
1 (10¾-oz.) can cream of chicken soup
1 cup milk
2 cups cubed rotisserie chicken meat
2 cups herb-flavored stuffing
½ cup sour cream
¼–½ tsp. pepper
¼ cup sliced almonds

1. Combine mushrooms, onion, and celery in 2-qt. microwave-safe casserole dish.

2. Microwave on High, uncovered, 5–6 minutes or until vegetables are tender, stirring once.

3. Remove from microwave and add soup, milk, chicken, stuffing, sour cream, and pepper. Top with sliced almonds.

4. Cover and microwave on High 10–12 minutes or until heated through. Let stand about 5 minutes before serving.

CHICKEN AND GREEN BEAN CASSEROLE

Melva Baumer
Mifflintown, PA

Makes 6 servings
Prep. Time: 35–40 minutes
Baking Time: 30–40 minutes

2 lb. frozen French-style green beans
2 Tbsp. butter
3 Tbsp. flour
¼ tsp. salt
Dash pepper
½ tsp. prepared mustard
1½ cups milk
½ cup mayonnaise
1½–2 Tbsp. lemon juice
4 cups cubed rotisserie chicken meat
½ cup freshly grated Parmesan cheese

1. Cook beans according to package directions. Drain.

2. Melt butter in saucepan. Blend in flour, salt, pepper, and mustard.

3. Over low heat, add milk, stirring constantly until mixture is smooth and thickened.

4. Remove from heat. Fold in mayonnaise and lemon juice.

5. Stir in chicken.

6. Spread bean-and-chicken mixture in greased shallow baking dish.

7. Spoon sauce over top of bean-and-chicken mixture.

8. Sprinkle with Parmesan cheese.

9. Bake at 350°F for 30–40 minutes, or until bubbly and heated through.

CHICKEN POTPIE

Lavina Ebersol
Ronks, PA

Makes 8 servings
Prep. Time: 45 minutes
Baking Time: 45 minutes

Filling:
3 Tbsp. butter
3 Tbsp. flour
1 tsp. salt
⅛ tsp. pepper
1 chicken bouillon cube
2 cups milk
1 (12-oz.) package frozen vegetables
1 cup chopped rotisserie chicken meat

Biscuit Topping:
2 cups flour
3 tsp. baking powder
1 tsp. salt
1 tsp. paprika
⅓ cup shortening
⅔ cup milk

1. Melt butter in saucepan. Stir in flour, salt, pepper, and bouillon cube.

2. Remove from heat and gradually stir in milk.

3. Return to heat. Cook, stirring constantly, until smooth and slightly thickened.

4. Add vegetables and chicken to sauce.

5. Grease 7×11-inch baking dish.

6. In good-sized mixing bowl, stir together flour, baking powder, salt, and paprika.

7. Cut in shortening with pastry cutter, or 2 knives, until mixture resembles small peas.

8. Stir in milk until mixture forms ball.

9. Roll out dough on lightly floured surface into 8×12-inch rectangle.

10. Fold dough lightly into quarters. Lift onto top of chicken mixture.

11. Unfold dough and center over dish. Pinch dough around edges of baking dish. Cut slits in dough to allow steam to escape.

12. Bake at 350°F for 45 minutes, or until pie is bubbly and crust is browned.

CHOPSTICK CHICKEN

Mary Ann Lefever
Lancaster, PA

Makes 4 servings
Prep. Time: 20 minutes
Baking Time: 40 minutes

---

1 (10¾-oz.) can cream of mushroom soup
1 (10¾-oz.) can cream of chicken soup
1 (5-oz.) can chow mein noodles, *divided*
2 cups chopped celery
1 cup chopped onion
3 cups chopped rotisserie chicken meat
1 cup cashews, salted or unsalted
1 small can mandarin oranges, drained
1 Tbsp. parsley

1. Mix together soups, half the noodles, celery, onion, and chicken in a large mixing bowl.

2. Place in greased casserole dish.

3. Bake at 350°F for 20 minutes.

4. Stir in cashews.

5. Return to oven. Bake 20 more minutes, or until bubbly and heated through.

6. Remove from oven. Top with oranges and sprinkle with parsley just before serving.

CHICKEN FRIED RICE

Makes 8 servings
Prep. Time: 20 minutes
Cooking Time: 15 minutes

1 oz. dried mushrooms
4 eggs, beaten
4 tsp. canola oil, *divided*
¾ cup diced low-sodium ham
3½ oz. green onions, sliced
4 cups steamed rice
½ can bamboo shoots, sliced
4 Tbsp. green beans, or more
1 cup diced rotisserie chicken meat
Salt to taste
Pepper to taste

1. Boil mushrooms in water to cover for 3–5 minutes until softened. Drain water and slice mushrooms.

2. Stir-fry eggs in 1 tsp. oil. Add ham and cook until heated through. Set aside.

3. Stir-fry onions in 3 tsp. oil.

4. Add rice, mushrooms, bamboo shoots, green beans, chicken, eggs, and ham. Stir-fry at least 5 minutes. Add salt and pepper to taste before serving.

CHICKEN CURRY

Tina Hartman
Lancaster, PA

Makes 8 servings
Prep. Time: 20 minutes
Cooking Time: 10–15 minutes

3 Tbsp. butter
¼ cup minced onion
1 ½ tsp. curry powder
3 Tbsp. flour
¾ tsp. salt
¾ tsp. sugar
⅛ tsp. ground ginger
1 cup chicken broth
1 cup milk
2 cups diced rotisserie chicken meat
½ tsp. lemon juice
Cooked rice, for serving

SERVING SUGGESTION:
Experiment by topping this recipe with mandarin oranges, cashews, coconut, peaches, bananas, olives, celery, tomatoes, onions, or cheese, individually or mixed as you prefer.

1. In a good-sized skillet, melt butter over low heat.

2. Sauté onion and curry powder in butter.

3. Blend in flour and seasonings.

4. Cook over low heat until mixture is smooth and bubbly. (This removes the raw flour taste.)

5. Remove from heat.

6. Stir in chicken broth and milk.

7. Return to heat. Bring to a boil, stirring constantly.

8. Boil one more minute, continuing to stir.

9. Remove from heat. Stir in chicken and lemon juice.

10. Serve over cooked rice, and with toppings for individuals to choose.

CHICKEN WITH QUINOA AND SPINACH

Karen Ceneviva
New Haven, CT

Makes 4 servings
Prep. Time: 20 minutes
Soaking Time: 1 hour
Cooking Time: 20–25 minutes

1½ cups raw quinoa

3 cups water

2 cups chopped rotisserie chicken meat

3 Tbsp. freshly squeezed lemon juice

2 Tbsp. extra-virgin olive oil

¼ tsp. sea salt

Pepper to taste, *optional*

2 cups fresh spinach leaves, well washed, dried, and chopped

3 large scallions, thinly sliced

3 Tbsp. fresh dill

1. Put quinoa in bowl. Cover with water and soak for 1 hour.

2. Drain, discarding soaking water. Rinse quinoa thoroughly.

3. In a good-sized saucepan, bring 3 cups water to boil over medium-high heat. Stir in quinoa.

4. Reduce heat to medium-low, cover, and simmer 15 minutes, or until all liquid has been absorbed.

5. Stir in chicken, lemon juice, olive oil, sea salt, and pepper if you wish.

6. Stir in spinach, scallions, and chopped dill.

7. Serve warm, or at room temperature.

CHICKEN AND QUINOA VEGGIE BOWL

Hope Comerford
Clinton Township, MI

Makes 4 servings
Prep. Time: 10 minutes
Baking Time: 15 minutes

3 bunches broccolini
2 cups cherry tomatoes
½ cup sliced red onion
¼ cup olive oil, *divided*
Salt to taste
Pepper to taste
2 cups cooked quinoa
2 cups chopped rotisserie chicken meat
2 avocados, sliced, *divided*

1. Preheat the oven to 375°F.

2. Trim 2 inches off the ends of the broccolini.

3. Between 2 baking sheets, spread out the broccolini. Arrange the cherry tomatoes and red onion around and between the broccolini.

4. Drizzle each pan of vegetables with 2 Tbsp. olive oil. Sprinkle each with the desired amount of salt and pepper.

5. Place in oven and bake for 15 minutes.

6. Divide the quinoa evenly between 4 bowls. Divide the chicken evenly between the 4 bowls.

7. When the vegetables are done, divide the vegetables evenly between the 4 bowls.

8. Top each bowl with ½ of a sliced avocado.

9. Eat and enjoy!

WHITE CHICKEN CHILI CASSEROLE

Zoë Rohrer
Lancaster, PA

Makes 8 servings
Prep. Time: 15 minutes
Baking Time: 30–35 minutes
Standing Time: 10 minutes

1 small onion, diced
1 garlic clove, minced
2 ribs celery, diced
1 green bell pepper, diced
1–2 tsp. oil
4 cups cooked white beans
1 cup chicken broth
1 cup sour cream, or ricotta cheese
½ tsp. salt
1 tsp. cumin
½ tsp. black pepper
1 (10¾-oz.) can cream of chicken or cream of celery
  soup
2 cups chopped rotisserie chicken meat
4 whole large whole-wheat tortillas, *divided*
2 cups shredded cheddar cheese, *divided*

SERVING SUGGESTION:
Great served with salsa.

1. In a large skillet, sauté onion, garlic, celery, and bell pepper in a bit of oil until soft.

2. Add beans, broth, sour cream, salt, cumin, pepper, and soup. Bring to a boil while stirring.

3. Remove from heat. Stir in chicken.

4. Spread ⅓ of chicken mixture in bottom of well-greased 9×13-inch baking dish.

5. Top with 2 tortillas, cutting them to fit the pan.

6. Spread on half of the remaining chicken mixture.

7. Top with half the cheese.

8. Follow with remaining 2 tortillas, a layer of remaining chicken, and a layer of remaining cheese.

9. Bake for 30–35 minutes, or until bubbly.

10. Let stand 10 minutes before serving.

MEXICAN CHICKEN STACK

Diann Dunham
State College, PA

Makes 6 servings
Prep. Time: 30 minutes
Baking Time: 25 minutes

1½–2 cups shredded rotisserie chicken meat
1 green bell pepper, chopped
¼ cup chopped onion
1 tsp. ground cumin
1½ cups chunky salsa
1 (3-oz.) package cream cheese, softened
1 (11-oz.) can Southwestern corn (mixture of corn, peppers, black beans), drained
3 10–12-inch flour tortillas, *divided*
1 cup shredded Mexican cheese, *divided*

SERVING SUGGESTIONS:
1. Pass extra salsa so diners can add to their individual servings if they wish.
2. Sprinkle chopped cilantro on top before serving.

1. Warm chicken, bell pepper, and onion in a nonstick skillet over low heat.

2. Stir in cumin and salsa.

3. Cook 2 minutes.

4. Add cream cheese and cook, stirring, 2 minutes until melted.

5. Stir in corn.

6. Spray an 8×8-inch baking dish with nonstick cooking spray.

7. Put 1 tortilla in dish. Stack in ⅓ of chicken mixture, and then 1 tortilla, ½ of remaining chicken mixture, and ¼ cup shredded cheese.

8. Add last tortilla, and remaining chicken mixture.

9. Cover with foil. Bake 20 minutes.

10. Uncover. Add remaining cheese.

11. Bake uncovered until cheese melts, about 5 minutes. Allow stack to rest 10 minutes before serving. Cut in wedges or squares.

TEX-MEX CHICKEN CASSEROLE

Ruth C. Hancock
Earlsboro, OK

Makes 6 servings
Prep. Time: 45 minutes
Baking Time: 35 minutes

2 cups shredded rotisserie chicken meat
2 cups crushed tortilla chips
1 (15-oz.) can beans, rinsed and drained
1 cup corn kernels
⅔ cup sour cream
½–1 tsp. chili powder, according to your taste
   preference
2 cups salsa, *divided*
1 cup shredded cheese, *divided*

1. Combine chicken, chips, beans, corn, sour cream, and chili powder in mixing bowl.

2. Grease 2-quart baking dish.

3. Layer half of chicken mixture into baking dish.

4. Top with half of salsa.

5. Top with half of cheese.

6. Repeat steps 3–5.

7. Cover with foil.

8. Bake at 350°F for 25 minutes.

9. Uncover and bake 10 minutes more.

QUICK AND EASY CHICKEN ENCHILADAS

Ellyn Nolt
Lancaster, PA

Makes 6–8 servings
Prep. Time: 20 minutes
Baking Time: 20 minutes

---

2 cups shredded rotisserie chicken meat
1 (15-oz.) jar salsa
½ cup (half an 8-oz. package) cream cheese, softened
12 flour tortillas
1 (16-oz.) jar taco sauce
2 cups shredded cheddar cheese

1. In large mixing bowl, mix together the chicken, salsa, and cream cheese.

2. Grease 9×13-inch baking dish.

3. Put about ¼ cup chicken mixture onto each tortilla and roll up.

4. Place filled tortillas side by side in baking dish, seam-side down.

5. Pour taco sauce evenly over top of rolls.

6. Sprinkle rolls evenly with cheese.

7. Bake at 350°F for about 20 minutes, or until filling is heated through and cheese is melted.

VARIATIONS:
1. Add 2¼-oz. can sliced black olives, drained, to step 7, sprinkling olives over rolls along with cheese.
2. Serve with shredded lettuce and chopped tomatoes as toppings.
3. Instead of cream cheese, use 1 cup sour cream.
Lavonda Hoover
Coatesville, PA

TIP:
You can customize this to suit your personal taste and that of those you're serving: the heat of salsa and taco sauces, the addition of onions, canned chilies, etc.

EASY CHICKEN ENCHILADAS

Lois Peterson
Huron, SD

Makes 4 servings
Prep. Time: 35–45 minutes
Baking Time: 40 minutes

1 (10¾-oz.) can cream of chicken soup
½ cup sour cream
1 cup picante sauce
2 tsp. chili powder
2 cups chopped rotisserie chicken meat
1 cup grated pepper Jack cheese
6 6-inch flour tortillas
1 medium tomato, chopped
1 green onion, sliced

1. Stir soup, sour cream, picante sauce, and chili powder in a medium bowl.

2. In a large bowl, combine 1 cup sauce mixture, chicken, and cheese.

3. Grease 9x13-inch baking dish.

4. Divide mixture among tortillas.

5. Roll up each tortilla. Place filled tortillas in baking dish, seam-side down.

6. Pour remaining sauce mixture over filled tortillas.

7. Cover. Bake at 350°F for 40 minutes or until enchiladas are hot and bubbling.

8. Top with chopped tomato and onion and serve.

QUESADILLA CASSEROLE

Lorraine Stutzman Amstutz
Akron, PA

Makes 8 servings
Prep. Time: 20 minutes
Baking Time: 15 minutes

2 Tbsp. olive oil
½ cup chopped onion
2 cups shredded rotisserie chicken meat
1 (16-oz.) can tomato sauce
1 (15-oz.) can black beans, drained
1 (15-oz.) can whole-kernel corn, undrained
1 (4½-oz.) can chopped green chilies
2 tsp. chili powder
1 tsp. ground cumin
1 tsp. minced garlic
½ tsp. dried oregano
½ tsp. crushed red pepper
8 corn tortillas, *divided*
1 cup shredded sharp cheddar cheese, *divided*

1. Heat the olive oil in a skillet. Add the onions and cook until translucent.

2. Add the chicken, tomato sauce, beans, corn, and chilies.

3. Stir in chili powder, cumin, garlic, oregano, and red pepper.

4. Bring to boil; simmer 5 minutes.

5. Spread half of the chicken mixture in greased 9×13-inch pan.

6. Top with 4 corn tortillas, overlapping as needed.

7. Top with half of the remaining chicken mixture and half of the cheese.

8. Top with remaining tortillas, chicken mixture, and cheese.

9. Bake at 350°F for 15 minutes.

CHIMICHANGAS

Lorene Good
Armington, IL

Makes 12 servings
Prep. Time: 25 minutes
Cooking Time: 20 minutes

---

1 Tbsp. olive oil
2 Tbsp. diced onion
2 Tbsp. chopped green bell pepper
2 cups shredded rotisserie chicken meat
1 (8-oz.) can tomato sauce
2 Tbsp. chopped garlic
Salt to taste
Pepper to taste
1 (16-oz.) can pinto beans
12 whole-wheat flour tortillas, 6-inch diameter

1. Heat the olive oil in a skillet. Add onion and bell pepper. Add the chicken, tomato sauce, garlic, salt, and pepper. Simmer.

2. Drain and mash pinto beans. Add to chicken mixture. Continue cooking on low heat.

3. Microwave prepared tortillas, one at a time, between 2 paper towels for 20 seconds each.

4. Fill each tortilla with about ⅓–½ cup sauce. Roll up and serve warm, or chill and serve later.

TAMALE PIE

Joyce Bond
Stonyford, CA

Makes 8 servings
Prep. Time: 25 minutes
Baking Time: 1 hour
Standing Time: 5–10 minutes

2 tsp. olive oil
1 medium onion, chopped
2 cups diced rotisserie chicken meat
1 garlic clove, minced
¼ tsp. salt
½ tsp. pepper
3 Tbsp. chili powder
1 (16-oz.) can tomato sauce
½ cup water
1 (15-oz.) can creamed corn
1 cup fat-free evaporated milk
½ cup egg substitute
½ cup yellow cornmeal
1 (6-oz.) can medium green or black whole pitted olives, drained, *optional*

1. Place olive oil and onion in 8-quart Dutch oven over medium heat. Cook, stirring frequently, until tender.

2. Add chicken to onion in Dutch oven. Stir.

3. Off the stove, stir in garlic, salt, pepper, and chili powder.

4. Stir in tomato sauce and water.

5. Add creamed corn, milk, egg substitute, cornmeal, and olives (if using).

6. Place Dutch oven, uncovered, in oven set at 375°F. Bake 1 hour until set.

7. Let stand 5–10 minutes before serving.

TIP:
Serve with pico de gallo and fresh cilantro.

BARBECUE CHICKEN SANDWICHES

Erma Martin
East Earl, PA
Janet Derstine
Telford, PA

Makes 8 servings
Prep. Time: 10 minutes
Cooking Time: 15 minutes

1 celery rib, chopped
1 medium onion, chopped
¼ cup chopped green bell pepper
1 Tbsp. oil
¼ cup brown sugar
¼ cup ketchup
¼ cup picante sauce
2 Tbsp. Worcestershire sauce
1 ½ tsp. chili powder
½ tsp. salt
⅓ tsp. pepper
Dash cayenne pepper
4 cups shredded rotisserie chicken meat
8 buns

1. In a large skillet, sauté celery, onion, and bell pepper in oil until tender.

2. Stir in brown sugar, ketchup, picante sauce, Worcestershire sauce, chili powder, salt, pepper, and cayenne pepper.

3. Bring to a boil. Reduce heat and simmer uncovered 3–4 minutes.

4. Add chicken. Simmer 10 minutes longer, or until heated through.

5. Serve on buns.

SOUPS & CHILIES

CHICKEN TORTELLINI SOUP

Mary Seielstad
Sparks, NV

Makes 4–6 servings
Prep. Time: 10–15 minutes
Cooking Time: 25 minutes

1 Tbsp. butter or margarine
4 garlic cloves, minced
5 cups chicken broth
1 (9-oz.) package frozen cheese tortellini
1½ cups diced rotisserie chicken meat
1 (14-oz.) can stewed tomatoes
1 (10-oz.) package frozen spinach or fresh baby
　spinach
½ tsp. pepper
1 tsp. dried basil
¼ cup grated Parmesan cheese

1. In large saucepan, melt butter and sauté garlic for 2 minutes over medium heat.

2. Stir in broth and tortellini and bring to a boil. Cover, reduce heat, and simmer 5 minutes.

3. Add chicken, tomatoes, frozen spinach, pepper, and basil and simmer 10–15 minutes. Stir every 3 minutes or so, breaking up frozen spinach, if using, or adding fresh spinach and stirring it into the soup.

4. Serve when soup is heated through, along with Parmesan cheese to spoon over individual servings.

CHICKEN BARLEY SOUP

Ida H. Goering
Dayton, VA

Makes 6 servings
Prep. Time: 20 minutes
Cooking Time: 1 hour

6 cups low-sodium chicken broth
1 ½ cups diced carrots
1 cup diced celery
½ cup chopped onion
¼ cup uncooked barley
2–3 cups diced rotisserie chicken meat
1 (14½-oz.) can diced tomatoes, no salt added,
   undrained
½ tsp. black pepper
1 bay leaf
2 Tbsp. chopped fresh parsley, or 2 tsp. dried parsley

1. Combine all ingredients except parsley in large kettle.

2. Cover and bring to boil.

3. Simmer, covered, for 1 hour. Stir occasionally.

4. Just before serving, remove bay leaf. Stir in parsley.

WILD RICE SOUP

Elaine Unruh
Minneapolis, MN

Makes 10 servings
Prep. Time: 15 minutes
Cooking Time: about 1 hour

1½ cups uncooked wild rice
3½ cups water
4 Tbsp. canola oil
2 Tbsp. minced onion
¾ cup flour
4 (14½-oz.) cans chicken broth
1½ cups diced rotisserie chicken meat
⅔ cup finely grated carrot
¼ cup slivered almonds
2 cups fat-free half-and-half

1. In a saucepan combine rice and water. Simmer for 45 minutes.

2. In a large soup kettle heat oil. Sauté onion until tender. With a wire whisk, stir in flour.

3. Gradually add chicken broth and cook until mixture thickens, stirring constantly.

4. Stir in rice. Add chicken, carrot and almonds. Simmer for 5 minutes.

5. Immediately before serving, blend in half-and-half.

CHICKEN RICE SOUP

Janeen L. Zimmerman
Denver, PA

Makes 10 servings
Prep. Time: 20 minutes
Cooking Time: 40 minutes

4 celery ribs, sliced thin
1 onion, chopped
2 Tbsp. olive oil
4 carrots, shredded
⅓ cup whole-wheat pastry flour
½ tsp. pepper
2 cups milk
4 cups raw wild rice
2⅔ cups raw brown rice
3 cups diced rotisserie chicken meat
3 Tbsp. chicken bouillon granules
8 cups water
2 cups grated cheese, *optional*

1. In a large stockpot, sauté celery and onion in olive oil.

2. Add carrots. Cook and stir 1–2 minutes.

3. Remove cooked vegetables from pot. Set aside.

4. Combine flour, pepper, and milk in stockpot. Bring to almost boiling, stirring frequently until thickened. Do not scorch or curdle milk.

5. Meanwhile, cook 2 kinds of rice according to package directions.

6. Add both kinds of cooked rice, chicken, bouillon granules, celery mixture, water, and cheese if you wish, to thickened creamy base in stockpot.

7. Cover. Heat thoroughly and serve.

SIMPLE CHICKEN & SPINACH SOUP

Carna Reitz
Remington, VA

Makes 4–6 servings
Prep. Time: 5 minutes
Cooking Time: 20 minutes

6½ cups chicken broth, *divided*
2 cups shredded rotisserie chicken meat
1–2 cups frozen chopped spinach or fresh spinach, chopped
Salt to taste
Pepper to taste
½ cup flour

1. Put 6 cups broth, chicken, spinach, and salt and pepper in a large stockpot. Bring to a boil.

2. Meanwhile, mix flour and remaining ½ cup broth together in a jar. Put on lid and shake until smooth. When soup is boiling, slowly pour into soup to thicken, stirring constantly.

3. Continue stirring and cooking until soup thickens.

CLASSIC CHICKEN NOODLE SOUP

Colleen Heatwole
Burton, MI

Makes 8 servings
Prep. Time: 15 minutes
Cooking Time: 30 minutes

2½ quarts chicken stock
½ cup diced celery
½ cup diced carrots
1 (8-oz.) package egg noodles
2 cups diced rotisserie chicken meat
Salt, if needed

1. Bring stock to boil in a medium-sized stockpot.

2. Add celery and carrots. Simmer for about 7 minutes, or until vegetables are tender but not overcooked.

3. Add noodles and chicken. Return soup to boil. Continue to cook another 5–7 minutes, or until noodles are tender but not mushy.

4. Taste for salt, and add only if needed.

GINGER CHICKEN NOODLE SOUP

Hope Comerford
Clinton Township, MI

Makes 8 servings
Prep. Time: 10 minutes
Cooking Time: 25 minutes

2 Tbsp. olive oil
2 carrots, peeled and sliced into ¼-inch thick disks
2 stalks celery, diced
1 cup diced sweet onion
4 garlic cloves, minced
2 cups shredded rotisserie chicken meat
2 bay leaves
2 Tbsp. freshly chopped thyme
1½ Tbsp. freshly grated ginger
1 tsp. salt
¼ tsp. pepper
8 cups chicken stock
1 (8-oz.) package egg noodles

1. In a large stockpot, heat the olive oil.

2. Sauté the carrots, celery, onion, and garlic in the heated olive oil until the onion is translucent and the vegetables are softened (about 7–8 minutes.)

3. Place the shredded chicken into the stockpot, along with the bay leaves, thyme, ginger, salt, pepper, and chicken stock.

4. Bring the contents to a boil and let boil for about 10 minutes.

5. Add in the egg noodles and continue to boil for approximately 10 additional minutes, or until the noodles have softened to your liking.

TIP:
Taste and make any necessary seasoning adjustments. You may need more salt depending on how salty your broth and rotisserie chicken are.

SPICY AFRICAN PEANUT SOUP

Rhoda Atzeff
Lancaster, PA

Makes 8 servings
Prep. Time: 15 minutes
Cooking Time: 40 minutes

1 tsp. sesame oil
1 cup chopped onion
1 large green bell pepper, seeded and finely chopped
2 garlic cloves, minced or pressed
4 cups chicken broth
1 (16-oz.) can crushed tomatoes, no salt added, undrained
½ tsp. red pepper flakes
1 Tbsp. curry powder
⅛ tsp. black pepper
1 cup diced rotisserie chicken meat
¼ cup uncooked brown rice
¼ cup smooth peanut butter

1. In large stockpot, heat sesame oil over medium heat. Sauté onion, bell pepper, and garlic until onion begins to brown.

2. Stir in broth, tomatoes, red pepper flakes, curry powder, pepper, chicken, and rice.

3. Simmer uncovered over low heat for 30 minutes, or until rice is tender.

4. Whisk in peanut butter until soup is completely smooth. Heat through.

STUFFED SWEET PEPPER SOUP

Moreen Weaver
Bath, NY

Makes 10 servings
Prep. Time: 20 minutes
Cooking Time: 1¼ hours

2 quarts tomato juice
2 cups diced rotisserie chicken meat
3 medium red, or green, bell sweet peppers, diced
1½ cups chili sauce
1 cup uncooked brown rice
2 celery ribs, diced
1 large onion, diced
3 chicken bouillon cubes
2 garlic cloves, minced

1. Add all ingredients to a large pot. Stir. Bring to a boil.

2. Reduce heat. Simmer, uncovered, for 1 hour, or until rice is tender.

EGG DROP SOUP

Kathryn Yoder
Minot, ND

Makes 6 servings
Prep. Time: 10 minutes
Cooking Time: 12–15 minutes

4 ½ cups water
4 chicken bouillon cubes
½ cup shredded rotisserie chicken meat
½ cup carrot, finely shredded
1 tsp. finely chopped fresh parsley, or ½ tsp. dried parsley
1 tsp. low-sodium soy sauce
2 egg whites, lightly beaten
4 tsp. scallions, sliced

1. In large saucepan, dissolve bouillon cubes in water over medium heat.

2. Add shredded chicken, carrot, parsley, and soy sauce.

3. Bring to a boil, stirring occasionally. Continue boiling, 4–5 minutes.

4. Slowly dribble lightly beaten egg whites into boiling soup, stirring constantly until the egg has cooked.

5. Serve with scallions as garnish.

SCRUMPTIOUS WHITE CHILI

Gloria L. Lehman
Singers Glen, VA
Lauren Bailey
Mechanicsburg, PA

Makes 6 servings
Prep. Time: 20–25 minutes
Cooking Time: 25 minutes

1 large onion, chopped
2 garlic cloves, minced
1½ Tbsp. oil
2 cups chopped rotisserie chicken meat
1 (4-oz.) can chopped mild green chilies
½–1 Tbsp. diced jalapeño pepper, *optional*
1½ tsp. ground cumin
1 tsp. dried oregano
1 (10½-oz.) can condensed chicken broth
1 (10½-oz.) can refilled with water
1 (15-oz.) can great northern beans
½ tsp. cayenne, or to taste
Salt to taste
6 oz. shredded Monterey Jack cheese
½ cup low-fat sour cream
Chopped green onions, *optional*
Fresh cilantro, *optional*

1. In large stockpot, sauté onion and garlic in oil over medium heat.

2. Add chicken, chilies, jalapeño pepper (if you wish), cumin, oregano, chicken broth, water, and beans to stockpot and stir well. Bring to a boil, reduce heat, and simmer, covered, 10–15 minutes.

3. Just before serving, add cayenne, salt, cheese, and sour cream. Heat just until cheese is melted, being careful not to let the soup boil.

4. Serve at once, garnished with green onions and cilantro if desired.

CHICKEN SALADS

APPLE CHICKEN SALAD

Marlene Fonken
Upland, CA

Makes 6 servings
Prep. Time: 30–40 minutes
Chilling Time: 2–12 hours

Dressing:
½ cup mayonnaise, or salad dressing
2 Tbsp. cider vinegar
2 Tbsp. lemon juice
2–3 Tbsp. Dijon mustard

2 cups chopped rotisserie chicken meat
2 ribs celery, chopped
¼ cup diced onion
1 green apple, chopped
1 red apple, chopped
⅓ cup dried cranberries
Salt to taste
Pepper to taste

1. Whisk together mayonnaise, vinegar, lemon juice, and mustard. Set aside.

2. Mix together chicken, celery, onion, apples, cranberries, salt, and pepper.

3. Pour on dressing and toss to mix. Refrigerate until serving. Flavor develops with longer chilling.

CHICKEN SALAD WITH BLUE CHEESE

Susan Smith
Monument, CO

Makes 4–6 servings
Prep. Time: 15 minutes

3 cups diced rotisserie chicken meat
6 cups shredded lettuce
1–2 cups mayonnaise
2 Tbsp. tarragon vinegar
4 Tbsp. chili sauce, or cocktail sauce
2 Tbsp. chopped green bell pepper
4-oz. blue cheese, crumbled
Whole lettuce leaves

1. Mix chicken with shredded lettuce.

2. Mix mayonnaise, vinegar, chili sauce, and bell pepper. Add crumbled blue cheese.

3. Gently combine chicken and mayonnaise mixtures.

4. Place salad in a bowl lined with lettuce or in individual lettuce cups.

TIPS:
1. White meat chicken is ideal for this salad.
2. The salad is best made and eaten on the same day.

ALMOND-APRICOT CHICKEN SALAD

Tracey Hanson Schramel
Windom, MN

Makes 6–8 servings
Prep. Time: 15 minutes
Cooking Time for pasta: 20 minutes

Salad:
½ lb. bowtie pasta, cooked, rinsed, and drained
3 cups chopped broccoli
2½ cups chopped rotisserie chicken meat
1 cup chopped celery
1 cup dried apricots, cut into ¼-inch strips
¾ cup toasted whole almonds
½ cup finely chopped green onions

Dressing:
¾ cup mayonnaise
¾ cup sour cream
2 tsp. grated lemon peel
1 Tbsp. lemon juice
1 Tbsp. Dijon-style mustard
1 tsp. salt
¼ tsp. pepper

1. In a large bowl, combine salad ingredients.

2. In another bowl, combine dressing ingredients.

3. Pour dressing over pasta mixture and toss.

TIPS:
1. Instead of stirring the almonds into the salad, sprinkle them on top if you like that look better.
2. Pass the dressing in a small pitcher so each person can put on the amount they like. The leftovers don't get soggy then, either!

FRUITED CHICKEN SALAD

Dottie Schmidt
Kansas City, MO

Makes 6 servings
Prep. Time: 20 minutes
Cooking Time: 20 minutes
Chilling Time: 2 hours

1 (6-oz.) package Uncle Ben's Long Grain and Wild
  Rice Original Recipe
1½ cups water
1½ cups diced rotisserie chicken meat, cold
1 cup mayonnaise
⅓ cup orange juice
1 cup sliced celery
½ cup chopped pecans
1 (11-oz.) can mandarin oranges, drained
½ lb. (about 2½ cups) seedless grapes, washed and
  halved
Romaine lettuce

1. Cook rice and seasoning according to package directions, except use 1½ cups water. Chill cooked rice.

2. When rice is thoroughly chilled, combine with remaining ingredients (except lettuce) in a large bowl, tossing very gently. Keep chilled until ready to serve.

3. Serve on a bed of lettuce.

FIESTA CHICKEN SALAD

Liz Clapper
Lancaster, PA

Makes 4 main-dish servings
Prep. Time: 25 minutes
Cooking Time: 10 minutes

2 heads Bibb or red leaf lettuce, or a combination
1 cup shredded carrots
1 medium tomato, diced
2 green onions, chopped
1 sweet red pepper
1 Tbsp. olive oil
1 cup thawed frozen corn
1 tsp. chili powder
2 cups diced rotisserie chicken meat
½ cup shredded cheddar cheese
8 Tbsp. ranch dressing
2 pita breads, 4-inch diameter, or flour tortillas

1. Tear up heads of lettuce and toss together in a large bowl. Top with shredded carrots, diced tomato, and chopped green onions.

2. Meanwhile, dice red pepper. Toss with olive oil and cook in a medium skillet over medium heat for 2 minutes.

3. Add corn and chili powder and cook for 1 more minute.

4. Top salad with diced chicken.

5. Spoon corn and pepper mixture over the top.

6. Sprinkle with cheese. Drizzle each salad with 2 Tbsp. dressing.

7. Grill pitas or tortillas for 2–3 minutes each side. Cut into fourths. Serve 2 wedges with each individual salad.

GREEK SALAD WITH CHICKEN

Gretchen Lang
Lockport, NY

Makes 4 servings
Prep. Time: 30 minutes
Cooking Time: 15 minutes

1 (6-oz.) package (about 6 cups) baby spinach, torn
6 cups romaine lettuce, torn
1 cucumber, chopped
1 red onion, chopped
3 tomatoes, chopped
½ red sweet pepper, chopped
1 carrot, shredded
1 rib celery, chopped
Pepper to taste
2 oz. (about ½ cup) feta cheese, crumbled
1 cup sliced rotisserie chicken meat
⅓ cup extra-virgin olive oil
⅓ cup rice vinegar

1. In a large bowl, toss all vegetables and pepper together.

2. Sprinkle cheese on top.

3. Place sliced chicken pieces on top of salad.

4. Mix oil and vinegar together in a small jar. Pour over all.

CHICKEN GRAPE PASTA SALAD

Hope Comerford
Clinton Township, MI

Makes 6–8 servings
Prep. Time: 10 minutes
Cooling Time: 1–2 hours

16 oz. penne pasta, cooked and cooled

2 cups cubed rotisserie chicken meat

1–2 cups halved grapes (green or red, or a mix of both)

½ cup chopped onion

Dressing:

½ cup mayonnaise

½ cup nonfat plain Greek yogurt

2–3 Tbsp. apple cider vinegar

2 Tbsp. sugar

1 tsp. garlic powder

1 tsp. onion powder

½ tsp. salt

⅛ tsp. pepper

1. In a large bowl, place the cooked penne, chicken, grapes, and onion.

2. In a small bowl, mix together the dressing ingredients. Pour this over the chicken and pasta mixture. Stir to coat everything well.

3. Refrigerate for 1–2 hours before serving.

EXOTIC CHICKEN SALAD

Mable Hershey
Marietta, PA

Makes 6 servings
Prep. Time: 30 minutes
Chilling Time: 2–3 hours

1½ cups slivered almonds, *divided*
1 lb. green seedless grapes, halved
4 cups chopped rotisserie chicken meat
1 (4-oz.) can sliced water chestnuts, drained
1 cup sliced celery
1½ cups mayonnaise
1½ tsp. curry powder
1 Tbsp. soy sauce
1 Tbsp. lemon juice
Lettuce leaves

1. Toast almonds by spreading them in a large dry skillet. Place over medium-high heat, stirring them frequently so they brown on both sides and don't burn.

2. Combine grapes, 1 cup almonds, chicken, water chestnuts, and celery in a large mixing bowl.

3. In a smaller bowl, mix together mayonnaise, curry powder, soy sauce, and lemon juice. Add to chicken mixture.

4. Chill several hours.

5. Sprinkle with remaining almonds.

6. Serve over lettuce leaves.

VARIATIONS:
1. Add ⅓ cup minced onions to step 3.
2. Replace mayonnaise, curry powder, and lemon juice with 1½ cups peach or lemon yogurt. Increase the soy sauce to 2 Tbsp.
3. In step 7, garnish prepared plates with melon wedges before serving.
—Donna Treloar, Hartford City, IN

CURRIED CHICKEN SALAD

Bonita Stutzman
Harrisonburg, VA

Makes 10 main-dish servings
Prep. Time: 20 minutes

1 cup mayonnaise
¾ cup plain yogurt
2 Tbsp. honey
1 Tbsp. lemon juice
1 ½ Tbsp. curry powder
6 cups chopped rotisserie chicken meat, cooled
3 cups halved red grapes
¾ cup toasted slivered almonds
¾ cup diced celery
Romaine lettuce

1. Mix together the first five ingredients in a medium bowl.

2. In a large bowl, toss together chicken, grapes, almonds, and celery.

3. Pour dressing over chicken mixture and toss.

4. Refrigerate until serving time.

5. Serve on a bed of romaine lettuce.

SIDES

ROASTED ASPARAGUS

Barbara Walker
Sturgis, SD

Makes 6 servings
Prep. Time: 5 minutes
Cooking Time: 12 minutes

1 lb. fresh asparagus spears
2–3 Tbsp. olive oil
⅛ tsp. pepper
2 Tbsp. balsamic vinegar

1. Place asparagus in bowl with olive oil. Toss together to coat asparagus.

2. Place asparagus spears on a baking sheet in a single layer. Sprinkle with pepper.

3. Roast uncovered at 450°F. Shake pan once or twice to turn spears after about 6 minutes.

4. Roast another 6 minutes, or until asparagus is tender-crisp.

5. Put on a plate and drizzle with balsamic vinegar. Serve immediately.

ROSEMARY CARROTS

Orpha M. Herr
Andover, NY

Makes 6 servings
Prep. Time: 15 minutes
Cooking Time: 15–20 minutes

1½ lb. carrots, sliced
1 Tbsp. olive oil
½ cup diced green bell pepper
1 tsp. dried rosemary, crushed
¼ tsp. coarsely ground pepper

1. In a skillet, cook and stir carrots in oil 10–12 minutes, or until tender-crisp.

2. Add bell pepper. Cook and stir 5 minutes, or until carrots and bell pepper are tender, but not too soft.

3. Sprinkle with rosemary and pepper. Heat through.

WHOLE GREEN BEANS IN GARLIC

Leona Yoder
Hartville, OH
Joyce Shackelford
Green Bay, WI
Doris Ranck
Gap, PA

Makes 4 servings
Prep. Time: 15–20 minutes
Cooking Time: 20–30 minutes

1 lb. green beans, ends trimmed
2 tsp. butter
⅛ tsp. finely chopped garlic
½ tsp. salt
¼ tsp. pepper
1 tsp. dried oregano, *optional*
⅓ cup shredded Parmesan cheese, *optional*

1. Cook beans in small amount of boiling water in covered saucepan until crisp-tender. Drain.

2. Melt butter in large skillet. Sauté beans and garlic in butter until heated through and done to your liking.

3. Season before serving with salt and pepper, and oregano if you wish.

4. Place in serving dish. Just before serving, top with shredded cheese if you wish.

CHEESY BROCCOLI CASSEROLE

Esther J. Mast
Lancaster, PA
Jan Rankin
Millersville, PA

Makes 6–8 servings
Prep. Time: 20 minutes
Cooking Time: 20 minutes

2 (10-oz.) pkgs. frozen broccoli
1 stick (8 Tbsp.) butter, melted, *divided*
1 (8-oz.) package Velveeta cheese, grated, *divided*
36–38 Ritz crackers (about ⅔ tube), crushed

1. Place broccoli in a medium-sized saucepan, along with about ¼ cup water. Cover and steam, stirring occasionally, until crisp-tender, about 5–10 minutes.

2. Drain broccoli and place in lightly greased 1½-quart casserole.

3. Pour half of melted butter over broccoli.

4. Stir in most of the cheese. Reserve the rest for sprinkling on top of fully mixed casserole.

5. In a mixing bowl, combine the remaining butter with the crushed crackers. Sprinkle over broccoli mixture.

6. Top with reserved cheese.

7. Bake uncovered at 325°F for 20 minutes.

QUICK STIR-FRIED VEGETABLES

Judith Govotsos
Frederick, MD

Makes 5 servings
Prep. Time: 20 minutes
Cooking Time: 7–10 minutes

4 garlic cloves, sliced thin
4 carrots, sliced thin on angle
1 small yellow squash, sliced thin on angle
1 small green zucchini squash, sliced thin on angle
1 large onion, sliced thin
1 Tbsp. olive oil
¼ tsp. salt
⅛ tsp. pepper

1. Prepare all vegetables. Do not mix together.

2. Place olive oil in large nonstick skillet.

3. Add garlic and carrots. Stir-fry 2–3 minutes.

4. Add remainder of vegetables. Cook and stir until just lightly cooked, about 5–7 more minutes.

5. Stir in seasonings and serve.

ROASTED SUMMER VEGETABLES

Moreen Weaver
Bath, NY

Makes 6 servings
Prep. Time: 20–30 minutes
Baking Time: 20 minutes

8–10 cups fresh vegetables: your choice of any summer squash, onions, potatoes, tomatoes, green beans, broccoli, cauliflower, carrots, green or red bell sweet peppers, mild chili peppers, eggplant, mushrooms, or fennel

Seasoning 1:
3 Tbsp. fresh basil, chopped
2 Tbsp. fresh cilantro, chopped
1½ Tbsp. fresh thyme, chopped
1 Tbsp. olive oil
½ tsp. pepper
3 garlic cloves, minced

Seasoning 2:
4 garlic cloves, minced
1 Tbsp. olive oil
2 Tbsp. fresh thyme
2 Tbsp. fresh oregano
2 Tbsp. fresh basil, chopped
2 Tbsp. balsamic vinegar
1 Tbsp. Dijon mustard
¼ tsp. pepper

1. Cut vegetables into bite-sized pieces for even cooking. For example, slice potatoes thinly, but chop summer squash in chunks. Place prepared vegetables in large mixing bowl as you go.

2. Toss vegetables with one of the seasoning options.

3. Spread seasoned vegetables in a thin layer on a lightly greased baking sheet with sides.

4. Bake in preheated oven at 425°F for 20 minutes. Stir occasionally.

OVEN FRIES

Sherry H. Kauffman
Minot, ND

Makes 6 servings
Prep. Time: 15 minutes
Baking Time: 25 minutes

3 medium unpeeled baking potatoes (1 ½ lb.)
2 large carrots
2 tsp. vegetable, or canola, oil
¼ tsp. salt
¼ tsp. pepper
Nonfat cooking spray

1. Scrub potatoes and carrots. Cut potatoes into 3½×½-inch strips. Pat dry with paper towel. Slice carrots lengthwise.

2. Combine oil, salt, and pepper in large bowl. Add potatoes and carrots. Toss to coat.

3. Arrange in a single layer on a baking sheet coated with nonfat cooking spray.

4. Bake at 475°F for 25 minutes, or until tender and brown, turning after 15 minutes.

BAKED SWEET POTATO WEDGES

Gladys M. High
Ephrata, PA

Makes 4 servings
Prep. Time: 15 minutes
Baking Time: 30 minutes

olive oil cooking spray
2 large sweet potatoes, peeled and cut into wedges
¼ tsp. salt
¼ tsp. black pepper
Oregano, thyme, rosemary, garlic powder, *optional*

1. Preheat oven to 400°F.

2. Coat baking sheet with olive oil cooking spray.

3. Arrange sweet potato wedges on baking sheet in a single layer. Coat with cooking spray.

4. Sprinkle potatoes with salt, pepper, and any additional optional seasoning of your choice.

5. Roast 30 minutes, or until tender and golden brown.

RANCH POTATOES

Charlotte Shaffer
East Earl, PA

Makes 8 servings
Prep. Time: 20 minutes
Baking Time: 1 hour and 10 minutes

6 medium potatoes, cut into ½-inch cubes
½ stick (4 Tbsp.) butter, cubed
1 cup sour cream
1 packet ranch salad dressing mix
1 cup (4 oz.) shredded cheddar cheese

1. Place potatoes in a greased 7×11-inch baking dish. Dot with butter.

2. Cover. Bake at 350°F for 1 hour.

3. Combine sour cream and salad dressing mix.

4. Spoon over potatoes. Sprinkle with cheese.

5. Bake uncovered 10 minutes until cheese is melted.

SOUR CREAM POTATOES

Renee Baum
Chambersburg, PA

Makes 6–8 servings
Prep. Time: 30 minutes
Cooking/Baking Time: 45–60 minutes

10 medium red potatoes
1 (8-oz.) package cream cheese
8 oz. sour cream
¼ cup 2% milk
2 Tbsp. butter, *divided*
1 Tbsp. dried parsley flakes, or 2 Tbsp. chopped
   fresh parsley
1¼ tsp. garlic salt
¼ tsp. paprika

1. Peel and quarter potatoes. Place in a large saucepan and cover with water. Bring to a boil.

2. Reduce heat and cover and cook 15–20 minutes or until tender. Drain.

3. Mash the potatoes.

4. Add cream cheese, sour cream, milk, 1 Tbsp. butter, parsley, and garlic salt; beat until smooth.

5. Spoon into a greased 2-quart baking dish.

6. Dot with remaining butter. Sprinkle with paprika.

7. Bake, uncovered, at 350°F for 30–40 minutes or until heated through.

MASHED POTATOES

Susan Kasting
Jenks, OK

Makes 6 servings
Prep. Time: 10 minutes
Cooking Time: 20 minutes

4 medium potatoes, peeled and coarsely chopped
4 stalks celery, coarsely chopped
3 whole garlic cloves
3 Tbsp. butter
½ cup chicken stock or milk

1. Place first 3 ingredients in a pot of water. Boil until potatoes are tender.

2. Lift out celery and garlic and place in food processor. Pulse until smooth.

3. Mash potatoes with butter. Add celery to mashed potatoes and mix together, adding milk/chicken stock as needed.

SCALLOPED POTATOES

Eleanor Larson
Glen Lyon, PA

Makes 6–8 servings
Prep. Time: 15–20 minutes
Baking Time: 1 hour and 15 minutes

¼ cup chopped onion
½ stick (4 Tbsp.) butter
¼ cup flour
1 ½ tsp. salt, *optional*
¼ tsp. pepper, *optional*
2½ cups milk
5 large potatoes, uncooked and sliced (your choice about whether to leave the skins on or not), *divided*

1. Cook onion in butter in a saucepan until tender.

2. Stir in flour, and salt and pepper if you wish. Blend well.

3. Gradually stir in milk, stirring constantly.

4. Cook until thickened and bubbly. Cook 1 minute more. Remove from heat.

5. Place half of sliced potatoes into a greased 2-quart casserole.

6. Cover with half the sauce.

7. Repeat layers.

8. Bake covered in a 350°F oven for 45 minutes. Stir.

9. Continue baking, uncovered, for 30 more minutes, or until potatoes are bubbly and brown.

CANDIED YAMS

Jamie Schwankl
Ephrata, PA
Alica Denlinger
Lancaster, PA

Makes 6–7 servings
Prep. Time: 5 minutes
Cooking/Baking Time: 40–50 minutes

---

1 tsp. salt
½ stick (4 Tbsp.) butter
¾ cup water
½–1 cup brown sugar, according to your taste preference
2 Tbsp. cornstarch
1 (40-oz.) can of yams, drained

1. Combine salt, butter, and water in a good-sized saucepan over medium heat.

2. In a small bowl, stir together brown sugar and cornstarch. Add to saucepan, mixing well.

3. Add the yams. Cook for 10 minutes, or until sauce starts to thicken.

4. Spoon potatoes and sauce into a lightly greased 2-quart baking dish.

5. Bake uncovered at 350°F for 30–40 minutes

RICE MEDLEY

Doyle Rounds
Bridgewater, VA

Makes 10 servings
Prep. Time: 5 minutes
Cooking Time: 20–25 minutes

1 cup raw brown rice
2¼ cups water
2 cups frozen peas, thawed
1 carrot, shredded
1½ tsp. salt-free herb seasoning
1 tsp. low-sodium chicken bouillon granules
1 tsp. lemon juice

1. In a large saucepan, combine first six ingredients.

2. Cover and bring to a boil.

3. Reduce heat and simmer 15 minutes, or until rice is tender.

4. Remove from heat and add lemon juice. Fluff with a fork.

HERBED RICE PILAF

Betty K. Drescher
Quakertown, PA

Makes 8 servings
Prep. Time: 15–20 minutes
Baking Time: 50 minutes

2 cups raw brown rice
1 cup chopped celery
½ cup chopped onion
1 Tbsp. olive oil
4 cups low-sodium, fat-free chicken broth
1 tsp. Worcestershire sauce
1 tsp. low-sodium soy sauce
1 tsp. dried oregano
1 tsp. dried thyme

1. Sauté rice, celery, and onion in olive oil in skillet until rice is lightly browned and vegetables are tender.

2. Pour into lightly greased 2-quart baking dish.

3. Combine all remaining ingredients in a bowl. Pour over rice mixture.

4. Cover and bake at 325°F for 50 minutes, or until rice is done.

RICE-VERMICELLI PILAF

Jan Mast
Lancaster, PA

Makes 4 servings
Prep. Time: 5 minutes
Cooking Time: 30 minutes

½ stick (4 Tbsp.) butter
1 cup uncooked long-grain rice
½ cup uncooked vermicelli, broken into short pieces
2¾ cups chicken broth
2 Tbsp. parsley

1. Melt butter in a saucepan. Add rice and noodles, stirring until browned, about 3 minutes.

2. Stir in broth and bring to a boil.

3. Reduce heat, cover, and simmer 20–25 minutes, or until rice is tender.

4. Stir in parsley before serving.

FRESH MEXICAN CORN SALAD

Hope Comerford
Clinton Township, MI

Makes 4 servings
Prep. Time: 20 minutes

1 Tbsp. butter
3 cups fresh or frozen corn kernels, thawed if frozen
½ tsp. salt
⅛ tsp. pepper
⅓ cup diced red onion
⅓ cup crumbled cotija cheese
¼ cup diced red pepper
¼ cup minced fresh cilantro
¼ fresh lime juice
1 Tbsp. minced jalapeño pepper
½ tsp. cumin
½ tsp. chili powder
½ tsp. smoked paprika

1. Heat a skillet and place the butter in the skillet. Once melted, add the corn, salt, and pepper.

2. Stir the corn frequently and cook 5–7 minutes, or until the corn is slightly charred.

3. Place the corn in a bowl, set aside, and let cool back to room temperature.

4. Once the corn has cooled to room temperature, add all of the remaining ingredients and stir.

5. Serve and enjoy!

CORN AND BLACK BEAN SALAD

Jamie Mowry
Arlington, TX

Makes 5 cups
Prep. Time: 15 minutes
Chilling Time: 30 minutes

4 medium ears uncooked sweet corn, kernels cut off
  (2 cups)
1 large red bell pepper, diced
½ cup thinly sliced green onions
½ cup chopped fresh cilantro
1 (15½-oz.) can black beans, rinsed and drained
¼ cup red wine vinegar
2 tsp. canola oil
1 tsp. sugar
½ tsp. garlic powder
½ tsp. ground cumin
½ tsp. freshly ground black pepper
Salt to taste

1. Combine corn, bell pepper, onions, cilantro, and beans in a medium bowl.

2. Whisk together vinegar, oil, sugar, garlic powder, cumin, black pepper, and salt.

3. Stir dressing gently into corn mixture.

4. Cover and chill for 30 minutes.

MARINATED ITALIAN SALAD

Tammy Smith
Dorchester, WI

Makes 6–8 servings
Prep. Time: 30 minutes
Chilling Time: 1 hour

1 cup baby carrots, sliced lengthwise
1 cup chopped sweet red pepper
1 cup chopped celery
1 cup diced, peeled jicama
1 cup diced zucchini
1 cup small cauliflower florets
½ cup chopped red onion
½ cup sliced green onion tops (use whites for another purpose)
1 (15-oz.) can black beans, rinsed and drained
1 (6-oz.) package pepperoni slices, cut in half

Dressing:
0.7-oz. packet Italian salad dressing mix, dry
¼ cup apple cider vinegar
3 Tbsp. water
½ cup oil
1 (8-oz.) package sharp cheddar cheese, diced or cubed

1. Place salad ingredients in large bowl.

2. Whisk together dressing mix, vinegar, water, and oil. Drizzle over salad. Toss to coat.

3. Chill at least 1 hour. Add cheese just before serving.

TIPS:
1. You may use any vegetables you wish. Try to use 7–8 cups of vegetables for 1 recipe of dressing.
2. Bacon bits, nuts, and seeds also work well if added just before serving.
3. Cubed pepperoni sticks or turkey ham can replace pepperoni slices.
4. For a change, serve this salad as a sauce over pasta.
5. Jicama is a Mexican vegetable with a mild sweet taste and a nice crunch. Look for it in the produce section of a big grocery store.

SPAGHETTI SALAD

Lois Stoltzfus
Honey Brook, PA

Makes 8 servings, about 5 oz. per serving
Prep. Time: 15 minutes
Cooking Time: 15 minutes
Cooling Time: 30 minutes

16 oz. angel hair pasta
¼ cup canola oil
¼ cup lemon juice
1 tsp. Accent seasoning
1 tsp. seasoned salt
¼ cup low-fat mayonnaise
1 green bell pepper, chopped
1 cup grape tomatoes
1 red onion, chopped
1 cup shredded 75%-less-fat cheddar cheese
½ cup sliced black olives
pepperoni, *optional*

1. Cook pasta according to directions.

2. Mix oil, lemon juice, Accent, seasoned salt, and mayonnaise together. Add to drained pasta while it is still warm.

3. When pasta mixture has cooled at least 30 minutes, stir in bell pepper, tomatoes, onion, cheese, olives, and optional pepperoni. Chill.

VEGGIE PASTA SALAD

Linda E. Wilcox
Blythewood, SC

Makes 4–6 servings
Prep. Time: 5 minutes
Cooking Time: 8–10 minutes
Chilling Time: 2–4 hours

8 oz. uncooked penne pasta
1 ½ cups cauliflower florets, or 1 ½ cups broccoli
  florets
1 ½ cups sliced carrots
1 ½ cups sugar snap peas
½–¾ cup light Italian dressing

1. Cook pasta according to package directions, adding the veggies to the saucepan 3 minutes before pasta is done.

2. Drain and run cold water over mixture to stop cooking.

3. Transfer drained pasta-veggie mixture to large mixing bowl.

4. Pour dressing over and chill 2–4 hours.

ROASTED RED POTATO SALAD

Mary Puskar
Forest Hill, MD

Makes 10 servings
Prep. Time: 30 minutes
Baking Time: 30–35 minutes

5 lb. red potatoes, skins on, quartered
1 lb. bacon
1 bunch spring onions, chopped
1 (16-oz.) jar Miracle Whip salad dressing

1. Bake potatoes at 425°F in a baking pan sprayed with nonstick cooking spray for 30–35 minutes, or until tender.

2. Meanwhile, cook bacon in a large skillet until crisp. Do in several batches so as not to crowd skillet. Drain bacon. When cooled, crumble. Set aside.

3. Mix all ingredients in a large mixing bowl. Toss well and serve.

CREAMY COLESLAW

Jane Geigley
Lancaster, PA

Makes 8–10 servings
Prep. Time: 15 minutes

---

1 head cabbage, shredded
1 medium carrot, shredded
1½ cups mayonnaise
2 Tbsp. milk
1 tsp. prepared mustard
1–2 Tbsp. vinegar
½ cup sugar
½–1 tsp. salt

1. In a bowl, mix together cabbage and carrot. Set aside.

2. To make dressing, mix together mayonnaise, milk, mustard, 1 Tbsp. vinegar, sugar, and ½ tsp. salt. Taste and add more vinegar or salt as desired.

3. Pour dressing over cabbage and carrot. Stir.

VARIATION:
Make a dressing with ½ cup milk, 3 Tbsp. mayonnaise or salad dressing, ½ cup sugar, ¼ cup vinegar, and a pinch of salt.
—Orpha M. Herr
Andover, NY

EXTRA INFORMATION

Abbreviations used in this cookbook
lb. = pound
oz. = ounce
pkg. = package
pt. = pint
qt. = quart
Tbsp. = tablespoon
tsp. = teaspoon

Assumptions
flour = unbleached or white, and all-purpose
oatmeal or oats = dry, quick or rolled (old-fashioned),unless specified
pepper = black, finely ground
rice = regular, long-grain (not Minute Rice or instant)
salt = table salt
shortening = solid, not liquid
spices = all ground, unless specified otherwise
sugar = granulated sugar (not brown and not confectioners')

Equivalents
dash = little less than ⅛ tsp.
3 teaspoons = 1 Tablespoon
2 Tablespoons = 1 oz.
4 Tablespoons = ¼ cup
5 Tablespoons plus 1 tsp. = ⅓ cup
8 Tablespoons = ½ cup
12 Tablespoons = ¾ cup
16 Tablespoons = 1 cup
1 cup = 8 oz. liquid
2 cups = 1 pint

4 cups = 1 quart
4 quarts = 1 gallon
1 stick butter = ¼ lb.
1 stick butter = ½ cup
1 stick butter = 8 Tbsp.
Beans, 1 lb. dried = 2–2½ cups (depending upon the size of the beans)
Bell peppers, 1 large = 1 cup chopped
Cheese, hard (for example, cheddar, Swiss, Monterey Jack, mozzarella), 1 lb. grated = 4 cups
Cheese, cottage, 1 lb. = 2 cups
Crackers (butter, saltines, snack), 20 single crackers = 1 cup crumbs
Herbs, 1 Tbsp. fresh = 1 tsp. dried
Lemon, 1 medium-sized = 2–3 Tbsp. juice
Lemon, 1 medium-sized = 2–3 tsp. grated rind
Mustard, 1 Tbsp. prepared = 1 tsp. dry or ground mustard
Oatmeal, 1 lb. dry = about 5 cups dry
Onion, 1 medium-sized = ½ cup chopped
Pasta: macaroni, penne, and other small or tubular shapes, 1 lb. dry = 4 cups uncooked
    Noodles, 1 lb. dry = 6 cups uncooked
    Spaghetti, linguine, fettucine, 1 lb. dry = 4 cups uncooked
Potatoes, white, 1 lb. = 3 medium-sized potatoes = 2 cups mashed
Potatoes, sweet, 1 lb. = 3 medium-sized potatoes = 2 cups mashed
Rice, 1 lb. dry = 2 cups uncooked

CONVERSION CHARTS

METRIC AND IMPERIAL CONVERSIONS
(These conversions are rounded for convenience)

Ingredient	Cups/Tablespoons/ Teaspoons	Ounces	Grams/Milliliters
Butter	1 cup/ 16 tablespoons/ 2 sticks	8 ounces	230 grams
Cheese, shredded	1 cup	4 ounces	110 grams
Cream cheese	1 tablespoon	0.5 ounce	14.5 grams
Cornstarch	1 tablespoon	0.3 ounce	8 grams
Flour, all-purpose	1 cup/1 tablespoon	4.5 ounces/0.3 ounce	125 grams/8 grams
Flour, whole wheat	1 cup	4 ounces	120 grams
Fruit, dried	1 cup	4 ounces	120 grams
Fruits or veggies, chopped	1 cup	5 to 7 ounces	145 to 200 grams
Fruits or veggies, pureed	1 cup	8.5 ounces	245 grams
Honey, maple syrup, or corn syrup	1 tablespoon	0.75 ounce	20 grams
Liquids: cream, milk, water, or juice	1 cup	8 fluid ounces	240 milliliters
Oats	1 cup	5.5 ounces	150 grams
Salt	1 teaspoon	0.2 ounce	6 grams
Spices: cinnamon, cloves, ginger, or nutmeg (ground)	1 teaspoon	0.2 ounce	5 milliliters
Sugar, brown, firmly packed	1 cup	7 ounces	200 grams
Sugar, white	1 cup/1 tablespoon	7 ounces/0.5 ounce	200 grams/12.5 grams
Vanilla extract	1 teaspoon	0.2 ounce	4 grams

OVEN TEMPERATURES

Fahrenheit	Celsius	Gas Mark
225°	110°	¼
250°	120°	½
275°	140°	1
300°	150°	2
325°	160°	3
350°	180°	4
375°	190°	5
400°	200°	6
425°	220°	7
450°	230°	8

INDEX

ABOUT THE AUTHOR

Hope Comerford is a mom, wife, elementary music teacher, blogger, recipe developer, public speaker, Young Living Essential Oils essential oil enthusiast/educator, and published author. In 2013, she was diagnosed with a severe gluten intolerance and since then has spent many hours creating easy, practical, and delicious gluten-free recipes that can be enjoyed by both those who are affected by gluten and those who are not.

Growing up, Hope spent many hours in the kitchen with her Meme (grandmother) and her love for cooking grew from there. While working on her master's degree when her daughter was young, Hope turned to her slow cookers for some salvation and sanity. It was from there she began truly experimenting with recipes and quickly learned she had the ability to get a little more creative in the kitchen and develop her own recipes.

In 2010, Hope started her blog, *A Busy Mom's Slow Cooker Adventures*, to simply share the recipes she was making with her family and friends. She never imagined people all over the world would begin visiting her page and sharing her recipes with others as well. In 2013, Hope self-published her first cookbook, *Slow Cooker Recipes 10 Ingredients or Less and Gluten-Free*, and then later wrote *The Gluten-Free Slow Cooker*.

Hope became the new brand ambassador and author of Fix-It and Forget-It in mid-2016. Since then, she has brought her excitement and creativeness to the Fix-It and Forget-It brand. Through Fix-It and Forget-It, she has written *Fix-It and Forget-It Lazy & Slow, Fix-It and Forget-It Healthy Slow Cooker Cookbook, Forget-It Cooking for Two, Fix-It and Forget-It Instant Pot Cookbook, Fix-It and Forget-It Freezer Meals, Welcome Home Cookbook*, and many more.

Hope lives in the city of Clinton Township, Michigan, near Metro Detroit. She has been happily married to her husband and best friend, Justin, since 2008. Together they have two children, Ella and Gavin, who are Hope's motivation, inspiration, and heart. In her spare time, Hope enjoys traveling, singing, cooking, reading books, spending time with friends and family, and relaxing.